Tai Chi Morning

Tai Chi Morning
Snapshots of China

Nikki Grimes • Ed Young

Cricket Books
Chicago

Library of Congress Cataloging-in-Publication Data

Grimes, Nikki.
  Tai chi morning : snapshots of China / Nikki Grimes ; drawings by Ed
Young.— 1st ed.
      v. cm.
Contents: Tai chi morning — Sweet deal — Laundry day — The pet —
Same difference — Street sweeper — Magic needles — Mongolian woman —
Downtown shopping — Waiting at the intersection — Huang Shan & the
Great Wall — The Forbidden City — View from a puffer-belly — Chinese
painting — Dinner guest — Lu Kaiti was his name — Tiananmen Square —
China's daughters — Itinerary.
  ISBN 0-8126-2707-5 (cloth : alk. paper)
  1. China—Juvenile poetry. 2. Children's poetry, American. [1. China—
Poetry. 2. American poetry.] I. Young, Ed, ill. II. Title.
PS3557.R489982T35 2004
811'.54—dc22

                                                        2003016506

For Gene and MaryLou Totten, who invited me on the journey of a lifetime.

—NG

For professor M. C. Cheng, who opened my eyes to the richness of Chinese culture and put me on a journey beyond anyone's wildest dreams.

—EY

Contents

独坐子

Introduction

Early in 1988, while living in San Pedro, California, I met Gene and MaryLou Totten, directors of FACE, an arts advocacy group. MaryLou asked me to help write plays for a team of FACE artists headed for China that fall. Once the scripts were completed, she invited me to audition for the team. I laughed, at first. How was I supposed to compete with the many talented performers living in Southern California, in Hollywood's own backyard? How could I even hope to make it through the auditions? After all, as a writer, I wasn't used to auditioning. Still, I thought it might be fun to try.

Boy, was I in for a surprise! That October, I found myself among a group of twenty artists boarding a plane for Beijing, China, for one of the most intense experiences of my life.

For three weeks, we toured six cities along the east coast of China, beginning in Beijing and ending in Hong Kong. We performed in Chinese theaters, taught seminars in Chinese universities, developed friendships with Chinese artists, students, teachers, and translators, and squeezed in a bit of sightseeing along the way. We even traveled into the interior, exploring areas of China few outsiders ever see. The China we saw was a mix of modern skyscrapers and ancient temples, of horse-drawn carts and sleek sedans. I caught glimpses of both Chinas when I was there in 1988. How much China has changed since then, I can only imagine. This collection of poems does not attempt to fill in the blanks. For that, you'll need to look elsewhere.

Tai Chi Morning is simply, as the subtitle implies, snapshots of China seen through the lens of a poet's eye. It is a collection of moments, a personal record of an outsider's first experience of China. Take it for what it is.

I think it's important to note that my tour of China came a few short months prior to the violence that took place in Tiananmen Square. While I was there, I felt the rumblings of discontent that led up to it. The tension was palpable, and it was a frequent point of discussion among my travel mates. Back home, I watched the news coverage of the event with horror, knowing that some of the wonderful students I'd met in the theaters I'd performed at and in the college classrooms I'd addressed were probably among those facing tear gas and military tanks. I looked at the slides of my friends and myself, smiling happily in a sun-dappled Tiananmen Square just weeks before, and I shivered, knowing that my memories of China would forever be punctuated by that uprising. I include a poem on the subject in this collection because my personal impressions of China would be incomplete without it.

I hope the poems in *Tai Chi Morning* whet your appetite. If they do, and you find yourself curious to learn more, plan a journey of your own. Travel to China through books, via the Internet, or by plane, and see what you can discover about the old China and the new.

Go on. What are you waiting for?

—*Nikki Grimes*

Since my family is in Beijing, I began my trips to China as soon as the U.S. began relations with the People's Republic of China. I recorded in my journal and sketchbooks the vast change that has taken place through the years.

The drawings in this book reflect life in China during the time when Nikki Grimes was traveling there.

—*Ed Young*

Tai Chi Morning

Beijing, the nation's capital, was the first stop on my tour of China. On one early morning walk, I passed a park where a group of men and women were practicing tai chi. I found it fascinating to watch because the exercises seem similar to modern dance, or even ballet. Tai chi is slow-moving, beautiful, and more complicated than it first appears, and so is Beijing! All in all, they are a perfect fit.

Tai Chi Morning

Early every morning
Chen Lai and her GongGong
slow dance with the warm wind
breathing as the earth sighs
arms brushing the airways
palms coaxing the sun's rise.
Chen Lai shadows GongGong's
graceful-as-a-cat step
as he dances
to the rhythm
of the heart.

■ *GongGong* is one Cantonese word for grandfather.

自行車

We zigzagged a lot on this trip, but in general we moved north to south. Nanchang was one of our southernmost stops. By the time we reached this city, we were homesick for all things American, including ice cream. There was no butter pecan or chocolate chunk to be found anywhere, so we thought we'd try something local—green tea ice cream. Yum!

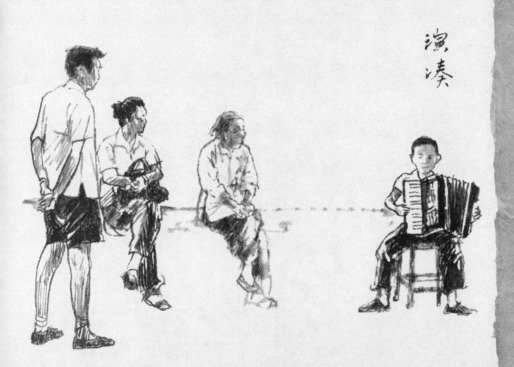

Sweet Deal

Bing Chi Lin
Bing Chi Lin

I need ice cream for breakfast.

Bing Chi Lin
Bing Chi Lin

Green tea flavor will do.

I'll feed the pigs
and sift the rice
and beat the mats
         if you only ask—

But first, I have to build my strength
with a bowlful of ice cream, or two.

The train ride from Beijing to Jinan revealed how stark the contrasts were between the old China and the new. Major cities like Beijing were dotted with skyscrapers outfitted with modern conveniences, while smaller towns and villages still found men balancing water jugs on poles across their shoulders and women washing linens by the river.

As we crossed the famous Yangtze River, I saw women on the banks beating clothing against the rocks. Peering at the site through the murky window of that creaky locomotive, I felt as if I'd stepped back in time. And in a way, I had. There I was traveling along a bridge that, for a moment, connected the old world with the new.

Laundry Day

With an ear tuned to Mei Li
Mother kneels over wet work

on the banks of the Yangtze
pounding grass stains and fresh dirt

from a basketful of clothes.
As she scrubs Father's white shirt

Mei Li asks her if she knows
that the train steamrolling by

carries travelers to a world
of spin wash & tumble dry.

Back in Beijing, I was reminded once again that we were no longer in Kansas! For instance, when was the last time you saw a gathering of old men holding court on a street corner, each accompanied by a pet bird in a bamboo cage? Taking a bird out for a bit of fresh air may have been a common practice in China, but it certainly seemed exotic to me. How could I not write a poem about it?

The Pet

One spring in Beijing
an old man with a bird
in a bamboo cage
went walking.
I can't guess the age
of the man or the bird
but I'm sure I heard
them talking.

清道队伍

Coal is a common source of fuel in China, and I breathed in massive amounts of its black smoke while I was in the North. More than once, I noticed men on horse-drawn wagons piled high with coal briquettes. They brought to mind the old men who sold melons from horse-drawn carts in the Harlem of my childhood, and so I decided to write about them. As for the city in the poem, I was never there. I chose the name from a map because the sound and number of syllables worked for the poem.

Same Difference

A Harlem honey,
I often woke to the sound
of the melon man
clippity-clopping
through town
on a horse-drawn cart,
spilling songs
and selling melons
on the way.

Then one day in Gansu,
a young man wheeled through
on a mule-drawn cart
groaning with coal
to warm the hearth.
He had no songs
to sing or sell,
only chatter.
But no matter.

For one magnificent moment,
strummed on the
strings of my heart,
Harlem and Gansu
ceased to be
a world apart.

Everywhere we went, I noticed gray-haired women in blue uniforms, sweeping the city streets. I tried to imagine my grandmother sweeping the streets of New York, but I couldn't. Still, she had something in common with the women of my poem. No matter how old she became, her hands were never idle.

Street Sweeper

Weary old woman of Jinan
dapper in uniform blue
nobody on this busy street
seems to notice you

swinging your sturdy broom
till memories swirl in the dust
moments when the younger you
tickled and cooed and fussed

over wiggling silk-bottomed babies
in strollers made of bamboo
or the sun-soaked afternoons
when you told your children "Shoo!"

and sent them out with a kiss
to run and romp and play
half a million years ago—
or was that yesterday?

I've been knitting ever since I lived in Sweden, so I'm always on the lookout for specialty yarns. One day, I came upon an old woman stationed next to a folding table piled with yarn, busily knitting a hat. She would stop only long enough to make a sale, or to take a sip of hot tea from a thermos. How I enjoyed watching her bamboo needles fly!

Magic Needles

Outside our front door
Grandmother props her table
of wool and silken yarns
for customers to buy.

Her fingers lightly flutter,
and dance with yarn and needle.
She keeps the silkworms busy.
"Slow down!" I hear them cry.

Sic-sic, sic-sic, sic-sic.
The bamboo needles chatter
as one sock, then another
appears between her hands.

Sic-sic, sic-sic, sic-sic.
Her joints grow cold and stiffen.
She sips hot tea to warm them
as passersby admire
the best socks in the land.

Hohhot, our second major stop in China, was cause for great excitement. It's located in Inner Mongolia, a region few Americans have an opportunity to visit. While there, I met a beautiful Mongolian mother and child whose features and clothing reminded me of Swedish Laplanders. Then again, they also reminded me of American Eskimos, which got me thinking about how interrelated we human beings are. It seems we're all connected somewhere down the line. Why is it that we only see our differences?

Mongolian Woman

She greeted me
on the streets of Hohhot
bundled in bright silks,
light dancing in her eyes.
She reminded me of an Eskimo.
No. Of a Laplander.
No. Of both.
Small wonder I felt as if
we'd met before:
same rose-round cheeks
same almond eyes
same pearl-white teeth
same smile.
Three women separated
by mile, upon mile, upon mile.
Identical triplets divided at birth?
Just how many tribal groups
are there on earth?
And who's keeping track?
And why?

Wangfujing is a great shopping center in Beijing. There you'll find stores like Shengxifu Hat Store, Yunfeng Leather Shoe Shop, and Wangfujing Department Store, which is chock-full of Chinese silk, Beijing arts and crafts, and jade. One way to get from store to store is by bicycle. You might get caught in a traffic jam, though!

Two-wheel traffic is a common sight in China. Most people use their bikes to go to school or to work each day. A street full of cyclists can be a bit overwhelming for an American, though. The only time we see that many cyclists is in a sporting event. That was my point of reference. I'd no idea where all those people were going. Three of my brave travel mates joined the throng on borrowed bikes, but I stuck with the tour bus!

Downtown Shopping

Near busy Wangfujing
bikers zing by in formation,
blocking cars and city buses
as they go,
knotting noonday traffic
row by row,

then screeeech to a stop,
grip their handlebars in
quiet impatience and hop
on the balls of their feet,
revving their engines,
astride leather seats,

black eyes fastened dead ahead,
coaxing the light-change
from amber to red
to green, and—THEY'RE OFF!
a cacophony of bike bells
breaching the air,

an onrush of racers
(black helmets of hair)
all in a hurry
pedaling—where?

停車場

Our tour took us to cities of varying size, but it was the big cities that felt especially odd to me. Standing at a major intersection one day, I figured out why. Chinese cities have very little racial diversity! Having grown up in the melting pot of New York City, the sameness of the hundreds of faces staring back at me was a shock to the system. I found myself feeling very uncomfortable at first. But then, as I noticed the smiles on some of those faces, especially the faces of children, my discomfort melted away. . . . And the longer I was there, the more I noticed the uniqueness of each face. How could I ever have imagined that any two were exactly the same?

佬
佬

Waiting at the Intersection

From where I stood
it was as if
God had run rampant,
cookie cutter in hand,
stamping out humans
with black hair,
almond eyes, sienna skin
in multiples of millions.
I hummed, hiding my
American discomfort,
then spun round searching
for a freckle-faced redhead,
or a blue-eyed blonde.
Not that I'm fonder
of fair skin or hair,
but there churned in me
a need to see
familiar differences.

So much of old China is sweeping and majestic. The Yellow Mountains and the Great Wall definitely top the list. I'm glad we visited the Great Wall during the first few days of our trip. I remember standing on those cobblestones, shading my face from the sun, and squinting at a wall that stretched as far as the eye could see. No wonder people say it's the only structure built by humans that can be seen from space! And yet, the Yellow Mountains have something to boast about as well, and so I imagined them being jealous of the attention given to the Great Wall. In this poem, I give the mountains a voice.

Huang Shan & the Great Wall

I, Huang Shan, am living, breathing,
deftly carved by Heaven's hand.
What makes you great, you wingless dragon,
wriggling lifeless through the land?

Why do many thousands flock
to stroll upon your stony path,
to gaze upon your chiseled rock?

Made by merely mortal men,
why do you draw cameras flashing
time and time and time again?

You lend no moss-bed for rest,
no steaming springs, no quilt of white
awaiting, sparkling, at your crest.

And yet, men marvel at you. Why?
Explain it to me, Brother River.
What is the mystery, Sister Sky?

Pardon me my consternation,
but I'm robed in orchid blooms.
Am I not due admiration?

Goddess flowers trim my sleeves.
In the autumn, like the maples,
I rain red and purple leaves.

Pine and camphor scent my spine.
Ginkgoes, firs, golden azaleas,
camellia blossoms—all are mine.

I am most worthy of amazement.
O, Great Wall, it's plain to see
from arctic peak to tropic feet
Mankind should honor me.

■ *Huang Shan* is the Chinese name for the Yellow
Mountains, a famous range in China known for its
lush and varied botanical life.

This tour gave me goose bumps. I'd just seen the Forbidden City in the film *The Last Emperor,* which was shown on the plane trip to Beijing. Yet not even the film was able to convey the immensity of the place. Passing through its great doors was definitely a "wow" moment. I felt like pinching myself to make sure I was really there.

歌
唱
鳥
籠
會

The Forbidden City

The Forbidden City
where royalty was once
hidden from view
is a place to tiptoe.
I follow the buzz of bodies
swarming over acres
of paved walkway
and greet a bronze lion
guarding the ancient temple.
I pat his burnished head,
close my eyes and hear
the footfalls of the last emperor
echoing through the courtyard.
His ghostly shape
waltzes in front of me.
He lifts a wavy finger
to his royal lips
and whispers
"Shhhhhhhh!"

We toured China by bus, plane, ferry, and rail. Train rides were the wildest, though. Each train trip ended with the crazy adventure of unloading ourselves and our props before the train took off. (Once, our props traveled on without us! Another train brought them back hours later.) Forget Amtrak! Chinese train travel was unlike anything I'd ever experienced.

View from a Puffer-Belly

If only we hadn't traveled by rail!
On this antiquated train, I cringe at the wail

of ear-splitting opera piped in near my head.
I groan and roll from a narrow bunk bed

so stiff my bones creak noisily.
A porter barges in with tea

as tepid as the cup is chipped.
The tablecloth is worn and ripped

and I'm all revved up to complain
until I glance out of the train

at teams of workers ankle-deep
in rice paddies who try to keep

the sun from scorching tender skin.
Then someone's grandpa, impossibly thin,

trudges by bearing barrels of grain.
(Was I really about to complain?)

A farmer plows with oxen in tow.
I look at him and suddenly know

I'm living a life of luxury.
I bow my head and enjoy my tea.

■ Puffer-belly is a name for an old-fashioned, steam-engine train.

室外書鋪

Our backpacks grew heavy as we were given works of art by Chinese artists we met along the way. Among them was a group of painters who let us watch them work. Our tour guide explained that a Chinese painter working in the traditional style may practice a brush stroke for years before he is considered a master. The work of such an artist may seem simple, but it is not. As a children's poet, I understand that all too well!

Chinese Painting

I watched a master,
who, they say,
practices painting every day,
the same stroke over,
and over, and over again,
capturing the essence
of magpie or mountain
in a handful of flourishes.
It is a poetry of watercolor
brief as haiku.
A few strokes
and a bird is born.
A few more
and it sings.

China's culinary practices are a mystery to me. I have no idea what the average person eats every day because, as a guest, I was routinely offered what turned out to be rare dishes and delicacies. Much of the food was quite tasty, but all of it was foreign fare and I was not always brave enough to try it. I'll bet first-timers to America feel the same way about our dishes! It's only natural.

Dinner Guest

I was a well-mannered
and most grateful guest
practiced my "Please"
my "Shé-shé" and "Yes,"

sampled the cockeyed
chicken-in-a-pot
wept pepper-red tears
the sauce was so hot,

sopped fisheye soup
with handfuls of bread
nibbled braised eel
(its tail or its head?)

I hissed at the sight
of barbecued snake
and serving me squid
was another mistake

but not 'til they brought
the Scorpion Sauté
did I and my appetite
scuttle away.

I'll never forget Hefei. Local news photographers and television reporters, thinking we were Hollywood stars, met us at the train. Two cast members did live in North Hollywood, but, as we tried to explain to the news crews, that is not the same as Beverly Hills. Besides, none of us was claiming to be Tom Cruise. Even so, photographers followed us everywhere. Lu Kaiti was among them. He tried to make up for our loss of privacy by giving us copies of photos he took backstage. Days later, as our train pulled out of the station, he slipped three of us envelopes with glorious photographs of the Chinese mountains at sunset. Mine hangs on the wall in my home, and every time I look at it, I smile.

Lu Kaiti Was His Name

He was a slip of a man
in sweater vest, jacket, and tie,
an Ivy Leaguer, from
the looks of him,
a bearded and mustachioed
cameraman from Hefei,
who knew no English.
Fortunately a photo
of mist over mountain
requires no translation
and it was this
he pressed into my hands
like an offering
as my train pulled away,
leaving little time
to do more than
mime my thanks,
hand over heart,
smiling a silent
Goodnight!
Goodbye!

The day I went to Tiananmen Square was warm and sunny. My friends and I were all smiles in the photographs we took. When I got back home and had my film developed, those pictures were among my favorites. Yet, every time I look at them now, I wonder how many of the university students I met in China were among those involved in the bloody revolt that took place in Tiananmen Square a few brief months after that warm and sunny day.

Tiananmen Square

A panda sculpted from greenery,
smiled and waved and offered me
a welcoming bouquet.
Sun blistered the portrait of Mao
and dappled the square that day.
Tourist chatter and peals of laughter
muffled shouts for democracy.
Death cries and the squeal of tanks
were a nightmare yet to be.
These days, I'm more than curious
about that cuddly bear.
Was he singed by the blaze
that scarred my new friends
one night in Tiananmen Square?

上火車遠遊

北京站

43

Hong Kong marked the end of our tour. It was a time to reflect on all we'd seen, and a time to pick up final souvenirs before returning home. One of my last purchases was a cloisonné bowl. The delicate yet strong work of art was a perfect metaphor for the Chinese women I'd met on this journey. They were small and delicate-looking, but they also had the sturdy backbone of a culture that is centuries old. Without a doubt, they have much to offer the world.

China's Daughters

Like fine cloisonné
they may appear delicate,
though one should not be fooled.
Fashioned by deft hands,
the brass of them is overlaid
by centuries of culture well-tooled.

■ Cloisonné is a decorative art made by laying enamel between metal wires.

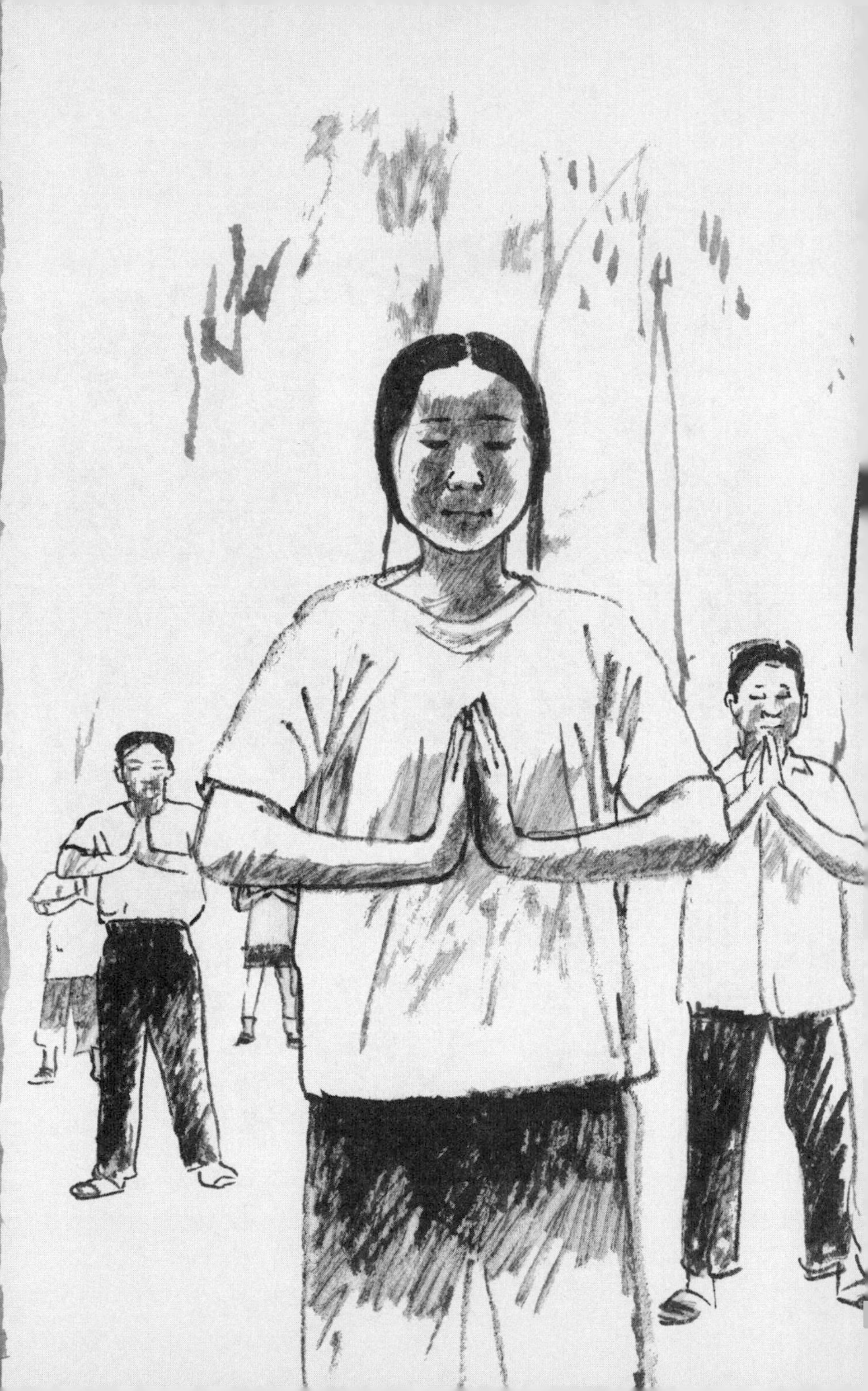

清晨練功夫

China Itinerary 1988

Date	Place	Carrier	Time	Information	Lodgings
Oct 11	Los Angeles	Flight 897	11:35 A.M.	Lv Los Angeles	
Oct 12	Beijing		7:05 P.M.	Ar Beijing	Beijing
Oct 13	Beijing			Ming Tombs & Great Wall	Bejing
Oct 14	Beijing	Train	5:00 P.M.	Lv for Hohhot	Overnight train
Oct 15			6:00 A.M.	Ar Hohhot University	College guest housing
Oct 15–18	Hohhot				
Oct 18	Hohhot	Train	5:47 P.M.	Lv Hohhot for Beijing	Overnight train
Oct 19		Train	10:38 A.M.	Lv Beijing/Ar Jinan 4:30 P.M.	
Oct 20	Liaocheng	Bus		Lv Jinan for Liaocheng	
Oct 20–22	Liaocheng				College guest housing
Oct 22	Liaocheng	Bus	A.M.	Lv Liaocheng for Jinan Afternoon tour of Jinan	
		Train	10:40 P.M.	Lv Jinan for Beijing	Overnight train
Oct 23	Beijing		7:10 A.M.	Ar Beijing: Tour Forbidden City Summer Palace, Heavenly Temple	

DATE	PLACE	CARRIER	TIME	INFORMATION	LODGINGS
Oct 24		Flight	7:50 P.M.	Ar in Hefei	College guest housing
Oct 24–26	Hefei			Sightsee	Hefei
Oct 27	Hefei	Train	10:35 A.M.	Lv for Yingtan	Overnight train
Oct 28		Bus	10:31 A.M.	Ar Yingtan/Nanchang	College guest housing
Oct 29–31	Nanchang			Sightsee	Nanchang
Nov 1		Flight	7:20 A.M.	Lv Nanchang/Ar Guangzhou	
			11:10 A.M.	Lv Guangzhou for Hong Kong	
			11:35 A.M.	Ar Hong Kong	YWAM guest dorm
Nov 2	Hong Kong			Sightsee	
Nov 3	Hong Kong	Flight 806	12:14 P.M.	Ar Los Angeles	

CHINA

Hohhot •   Bejing

Liaocheng •   Jinan

Hefei •

Yingtan

Nanchang

Guangzhou

Hong Kong

独坐子 only son *(pg. viii)*

自行車 bicyclers *(pg. 3)*

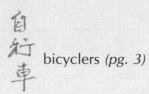

演奏 musical performance *(pg. 4)*

馬騾子車 mule cart *(pg. 6)*

靖道隊伍 street cleaning squadron *(pg. 9)*

觀棋不語 chess game *(pg. 12)*

耕田水牛 tilling in the wet field *(pg. 14)*

閱讀 reading *(pg. 16)*

停車場 parking lot *(pgs. 20-21)*

佬佬 old woman *(pg. 22)*

下輪船 passengers disembarking *(pg. 27)*

歌啼鳥龐會 singing birds club *(pg. 28)*

室外書鋪 outdoor library *(pg. 32-33)*

馬驢車 mule cart and bicyclers *(pg. 34)*

拉麵 noodle shop *(pg. 37)*

收垃圾人 trash collector *(pg. 38)*

上火車遠遊 train station in Beijing *(pg. 42-43)*

清晨練功夫 kung fu in the park *(pg. 46-47)*